STORIES FROM THE BIBLE

THE NEW TESTAMENT

First published in this edition in 2007 by Evans Brothers Ltd.,
2A Portman Mansions, Chiltern St, London W1U 6NR

Created and produced by Rachel Coombs, Nicholas Harris, Sarah
Hartley and Erica Simms, Orpheus Books Ltd.

Text by Olivia Brookes

Consultant: Robert Willoughby, London School of Theology, Middlesex,
England

Illustrated by Nicki Palin

ISBN 978-0-237534-58-5

Printed and bound in China.

Evans

British Library Cataloguing in Publication Data

Brookes, Olivia
    The New Testament. - (Stories from the Bible)
    1. Bible stories, English - N.T - Juvenile literature
    I. Title II. Palin, Nicki
    226'.09505

ISBN-13: 9780237534585

STORIES FROM THE BIBLE

THE NEW TESTAMENT

Illustrated by Nicki Palin

Evans

Contents

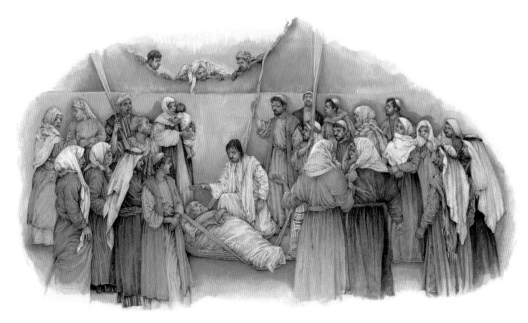

Introduction

FEW LIFE STORIES are as well known as that of Jesus Christ. In this book you will find a selection of stories from Jesus's life and learn about His teachings about humanity and God. Read about His birth, the miracles He performed, the people He healed and about His death and resurrection. You will also find stories about His disciple Paul's incredible journeys to spread His teachings around the world.

The Annunciation

MARY was just an ordinary girl. She was very faithful to God. Her parents had arranged for her to marry a local carpenter called Joseph. But one day something extraordinary happened. While Mary was saying her prayers, the angel Gabriel appeared before her. He told her not to be afraid. He had been sent by God to tell her something wonderful. Mary had been chosen to be the mother of God's son. She was to call Him Jesus.

The birth of Jesus

JUST before Mary's baby was due, the Roman
Emperor Augustus ordered everyone in the Empire
to return to their home town. Joseph was from
Bethlehem so he took Mary there. It was a long
journey from Nazareth.

WHEN Mary and Joseph arrived, the town was already full of people. There was nowhere to stay. Mary and Joseph took shelter in a stable. That night, Mary's baby was born. In the hills around Bethlehem some shepherds were looking after their sheep. Suddenly, the sky shone with a bright light and a chorus of angels sang. The shepherds hurried to the stable to see the baby Jesus.

A FEW months later, three strangers from far away in the east arrived in Bethlehem. They had seen a new star in the sky and followed it. These three wise men gave Jesus gifts of gold, frankincense and myrrh.

Jesus's early life

A S A BOY, Jesus went to the temple in Jerusalem for Passover. When it was over, his family left to return to Nazareth. But Mary could not find Jesus anywhere. Eventually, she found her son talking to the elders in the temple. She was surprised that, though He was young and training to be a carpenter with Joseph, He was able to discuss Jewish law with scholars.

JESUS'S cousin, John the Baptist, preached to people who lived in the desert around the River Jordan. He baptized them in the river to cleanse them from their sins. One day, Jesus asked John to baptize him. John did not consider himself worthy, but Jesus insisted. As He emerged from the water a voice came from heaven and the Holy Spirit came to Him in the form of a dove.

JESUS went into the Judean desert where He stayed for forty days and forty nights. There, Satan tempted Him. Satan told Him to turn the rocks into bread, but Jesus would not. Then Satan took Him to a high hill. If Jesus would obey him, Satan would give Him all that He saw. Jesus would not. Finally Satan took Jesus to a cliff and told Him to jump; surely the angels would catch Him. Jesus refused and Satan left. Jesus had passed God's test.

The miracles of Jesus

JESUS returned to Galilee and began to spread the word of God. One night, he was preaching to people by the Sea of Galilee, when he saw two fishermen cleaning their nets. The beach had become too crowded so he asked the men, Simon Peter and his brother Andrew, if they could row him out a little way offshore so he could speak to the crowd more easily. The men agreed. After Jesus had finished speaking, He told the fishermen to cast their nets. They obeyed, even though they had caught no fish that night. They were rewarded with more fish than their boats could hold. The men left everything and followed Jesus as His disciples.

JESUS performed many miracles. He showed people that God was amongst them. One of these miracles took place at a house in Capernaum. Jesus was preaching to a crowd, among whom were some Pharisees. A group of friends had brought a paralyzed man to be healed. By now the house was so crowded they could not get in through the door. So they lowered him down through the roof. Touched by their faith, Jesus told the man that his sins were forgiven and that he should rise up and walk. The man walked and the crowd was amazed. The Pharisees were angry and accused Jesus of blasphemy.

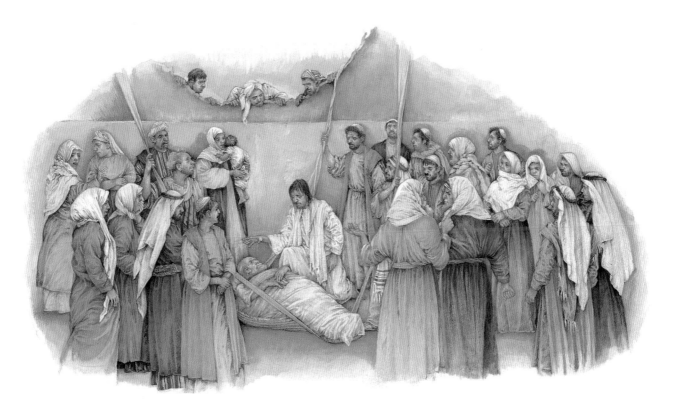

Teaching and healing

WHEN Jesus and His disciples were crossing the Sea of Galilee, a storm rose up. The disciples were terrified. The boat started to fill with water. Fearing they were going to drown, they woke Jesus. Jesus commanded the wind and water to be calm, and the storm subsided. He chided his disciples for their lack of faith. The disciples were in awe of this man who was obeyed even by the wind and the waves.

JESUS ONCE gave a sermon on a mountainside, so that everyone could hear him. He told the crowd that anyone who had faith in Him, no matter how poor or humble, would be welcomed into heaven.

A LARGE crowd gathered around Jesus. Among them was an official from the synagogue named Jairus. His daughter was very ill and he asked Jesus to come and save her. Jesus went to Jairus's house but when He arrived, a servant told Him that the little girl had already died. Jesus told Jairus to have faith; she was only sleeping. He held her hand and told her to get up. She sat up and then walked around. Her parents were amazed. Jesus asked them not to tell anyone what they had seen.

Feeding the five thousand

JESUS and His disciples spent nearly all their time teaching people about God. One day they crossed the Sea of Galilee to find some rest but the crowd followed them. Despite His exhaustion, Jesus began to speak to them. It was late and the place where they had stopped was remote. The disciples asked Jesus to send the crowd away to find food but He replied that the disciples themselves could feed the people. Following Jesus's instructions, the disciples gathered all the food they had: two fish and five loaves of bread. Jesus blessed the food and the disciples handed it out. The food multiplied and all five thousand ate as much as they wanted.

AFTERWARDS, Jesus sent the disciples out in their boat across the Sea of Galilee. The crowds eventually went home. Later that evening, the disciples saw what they thought was a ghost walking on the water towards them. Peter saw that it was Jesus. He stepped out of the boat and walked to Him. Peter realised that he needed only faith to make such incredible things happen.

The good Samaritan

MOST of Jesus's ministry was spent in Galilee but He knew the time was coming when He would go up to heaven. He set out for Jerusalem. On the way, Jesus told a story about a man who had been attacked and robbed. The thieves left him badly hurt by the side of the road. A priest and a Levite passed by, but neither helped. Then a Samaritan saw the man. He stopped, bandaged the injuries and took the man to an inn. The Jews and Samaritans did not like each other but Jesus taught that people should care for one another despite their differences.

WHEN people brought their children to Jesus, the disciples tried to turn them away, fearing they would annoy Him. But Jesus stopped the disciples and bent down among the children. He blessed them and told the disciples not to prevent children from coming to Him. He said that the kingdom of heaven belonged to them. The children were able to trust in Jesus and have a simple, unquestioning faith.

Lazarus comes back to life

I N A TOWN called Bethany there lived two sisters, Mary and Martha, and their brother, Lazarus. Jesus had stayed with them many times while He was travelling. One day Lazarus fell ill. The sisters sent a message to Jesus. But when Jesus arrived Lazarus had already been dead for four days. Jesus wept with the sisters. He went to see the tomb and asked for the entrance stone to be rolled away. Martha objected but Jesus told her to have faith. They rolled the stone away and, after praying to God, Jesus called out to Lazarus. The dead man walked out of the tomb alive, still bound in funeral cloths.

THERE was a man called Zacchaeus in Jericho. He was a dishonest tax collector who kept much of the money he collected for himself. When Jesus came to Jericho, Zacchaeus climbed a tree to hear Him speak. Jesus called him down and asked to stay at his house. Zacchaeus was surprised. Many people were angry that Jesus would favour such a sinner. But Jesus's influence changed him into a generous and honest man.

THE PHARISEES often asked Jesus difficult questions. They were trying to make Him say something that was against Jewish law so that He could be arrested. Each time Jesus would calmly respond, often quoting their own Scriptures. They could find nothing to use against Him.

Jesus arrives in Jerusalem

NEWS spread that Jesus was going to Jerusalem for the Passover. Crowds began to gather. Hearing this, Jesus sent his disciples to look for a young donkey. They found one tethered to a doorway. He rode into Jerusalem on its back. The crowds waved palm leaves and laid their coats down in front of Him. They shouted "Hosanna! Blessed is He who comes in the name of the Lord." The Pharisees could not believe their eyes. Jesus was being welcomed as a Messiah, or Saviour. They told each other that Jesus must be stopped.

ONCE He arrived in Jerusalem, Jesus went to
the temple to pray. The temple was full of
people selling animals and other goods.
Here, people also borrowed money from money-
lenders. Jesus was furious. He overturned their tables
and drove the traders out of the temple. He said,
"Take these things out of my Father's house. It is a
house of prayer, not a robbers' den."

The Last Supper

JESUS ate the Passover meal with His disciples in the upper room of a small house in Jerusalem. As they were eating, He turned to them and told them that one of the disciples would betray Him. Each disciple protested he would never betray Jesus, including Judas. Jesus took some bread and wine. He blessed it and gave it to the disciples. It was, He said, a sign of His promise to the world that He would save them.

JESUS went to the Garden of Gethsemane to pray. Not long after, Judas arrived with guards armed with swords and clubs. Judas went up to Jesus and greeted Him with a kiss. It was his sign to the guards that this was the man they were looking for. The guards arrested Jesus and took Him away to be tried.

Simon Peter and another disciple followed the guards to the high priest's house. While they were waiting outside, one of the servants asked Peter if he was one of Jesus's disciples. Peter said no. This happened three times during the night, as Jesus had earlier predicted. Peter realized in the morning how afraid he had been. His fear made him hide his faith and he was ashamed of himself.

Death and resurrection

JESUS was brought before the religious leaders. They sentenced Him to death, but they did not have the power to execute Him. They took him to the Roman governor, Pontius Pilate. Pilate questioned Jesus but could find nothing to condemn Him as a criminal. So, because it was festival time, he offered to release Jesus. But the citizens of Jerusalem shouted to Pilate to crucify Him. Pilate relented and handed Jesus over to the guards.

JESUS was nailed to a cross between two criminals. A crown of thorns cut into His forehead. His mother Mary, his disciple John and Mary Magdalene wept at His feet. Jesus asked God to forgive His executioners. After much suffering, He cried out to God. At the moment of His death the sky became dark and there was a great earthquake.

JESUS'S body was wrapped in a linen sheet and placed in a cave. A large stone was rolled across its entrance. But later, when two friends of Jesus, Mary and Mary Magdalene, went to the tomb, the stone had been rolled away and the body had gone. Two angels told them that Jesus had been raised from the dead.

LATER that day, two of the disciples trudged sadly towards the village of Emmaus. A stranger joined them. They told him about Jesus. The stranger went with them to Emmaus and shared a meal with them. It was not until he broke the bread and blessed it that the disciples recognized the stranger as Jesus.

JESUS gathered His disciples together for the last time. After blessing them, He was lifted up into heaven in a dazzling cloud. Two angels appeared before the disciples. They told the men that Jesus would one day return in glory.

The travels of Paul

AFTER Jesus ascended into heaven, the disciples began spreading the good news that He had risen from the dead. Saul was a Pharisee who hated Jesus's followers. He arrested and imprisoned many of them.

One day, on his way to Damascus, a bright light blinded him and God spoke to him. After this, he followed Jesus and spread His word.

SAUL changed his name to Paul as a sign of his conversion. On his first journey, he visited Antioch with the disciple Barnabas. Some of the people they spoke to became Christians.

DURING Paul's second journey, he was imprisoned in Philippi with his companion Silas. That night, an earthquake shook the prison and the walls fell down. The jailer thought the prisoners had escaped, so he prepared to kill himself in shame. But Paul called to him, "Do not harm yourself, for we are all still here." Moved by the power of God, the jailer fell on his knees before Paul.

Paul's journey to Rome

WHEN Paul returned to Jerusalem, he was attacked by a mob and arrested. The mob was angry because they thought Paul was trying to encourage people to abandon the Jewish faith. After a trial in Caesarea, Paul was sent to Rome to appear before the Emperor Nero.

ON THE WAY to Rome, the ship carrying Paul and the other prisoners was caught in a terrible storm. Paul assured everyone on board that God would not let them come to harm. When the boat was shipwrecked near Malta, everyone escaped alive. Paul performed miracles and preached to his fellow prisoners, guards and the people of Malta.

AFTER his trial, Paul was held in a
private house. He was under arrest but
he was still allowed a certain amount
of freedom. It was here that Paul wrote to the
many people he had met on his travels. He
encouraged them to spread the word and told
them always to have faith.

Index